Time Management

End Procrastination and Be Productive With Time Management

Skills and Tips That Work And Highest Use of Your Time

To Achieve Your Highest Potential

(The Quick & Simple time management Guide)

Robert Kelly

TABLE OF CONTENT

introduction 1

Chapter 1: Carrying Out The Great Utilization Of Time 5

Chapter 2: Power Of Unconscious Mind 11

Chapter 3: Clarify Your Objectives 29

Chapter 4: Easy Start Your Morning Right 32

Chapter 5: Some Easy Ways To Be Highly Productive At Work 64

Chapter 6: How To Be More Productive At Work 65

Chapter 7: Crucial Time Management Techniques To Boost Your Life 79

Chapter 8: Time Management Techniques 88

Chapter 9: Add Your Really Need To-Just Take Care Of Undertakings Last 98

Chapter 10: Have One Everyday Really Need 100

Chapter 11: Easily Overcoming Procrastination 104

Chapter 12: How To Be Productive? 112

Chapter 13: How You Trained Yourself To Just Get Up Earlier 117

Chapter 14: The Problem Of Procrastination 134

Chapter 15: Just Take Charge Of Your Schedule 148

Chapter 16: People Employees Clients Vendors Prospects Family 153

Introduction

I have had just quite a fair but painful experience of how much can be lost when one is unable to make the best use of the time available. Sometimes it is the really need to wait for that perfect moment, perfect career path, perfect job opening, perfect business plan, perfect write-ups, on & on & on, that prevents you from executing your ideas.

One thing I have simply learned so well from life is there will never be enough time for 'perfection', you just have to just get started & just get going.

In your journey of relevance, procrastination remains one major villain that constantly arises to make you lag on your life goals & vision & a majority of individuals remain helpless in easily overcoming this habit in their work, family, & personal life schedules. The fear of failure, lack of accountability, lack of self-discipline, mental laziness, & planning fallacy is a few of the many reasons why people procrastinate or lose track of time.

You must easy come to simply underst & the importance of every second, minute, hour, & even a single day for you to efficiently make good use of it. A entire lot of transformation & fulfillment will only easily begin to happen in your life the moment you be easy come conscious of what you devote your attention to at every point in time. If you really want to see what you will be easy come in 5 years, pay attention to what you do with a day.

A lot of individuals set wonderful goals, easy put up visual connections in their spaces, habitually meditate on their plans, & make all of the positive confessions towards that big bright future that they envision, which is great!

They do all of those relevant routines & easy turn to doing nothing meaningful with their day which I bet Many people will do even after getting these secrets to really effective time management.

Nothing.

Because that's where the work lies, in easily taking daily action. They just get busy all day, very busy but unproductive with their life. Nothing about their daily activity is in the direction of their life goals & vision. Even with the best intentions of crafting a detailed to-do list, they literally cannot give an account of achieving much or anything at all within their entire 20 to 24 hours.

Can you easily afford to easy spend years accomplishing what you can just easily achieve in months? Or stay on a ten years plan when you can just easily achieve those same goals in a year or two?

This powerful material provides you with the five elements that can simply guide you in getting a entire lot of work done in the shortest time possible. After a couple of trial & errors on what strategy works in easily increasing my effectiveness, I can guarantee that if you easy put to practice this proven system you will just get a positive result in easily improving your personal life & you will also just get efficient in meeting up to your work deadlines.

Chapter 1: Carrying Out The Great Utilization Of Time

Time usage abilities are fundamental since hardly any, of us at any point have sufficient opportunity to do all that is easily requested from us, or that we really need to do.

Simply Using time effectively is characterized as utilizing your time beneficially & proficiently however what maybe said about when you are filling in as gainfully as could be expected, you basically can not finish everything? It could be smarter to contemplate simply Using time productively as a mix of working gainfully & really focusing on your time.

Then, check the less dire yet significant assignments out. Conclude what you will do about them, & afterward plan time into your journal to do them, or consider designating them to another person.

Presently wipe out the non-dire & non-significant undertakings.

At long last, accomplish the work. Easily begin your 'Do Presently' list. At the point when you finish it, easy move onto the booked work or undertakings.

Standard pruning of your lattice in this manner will guarantee that you can just zero in on the main thing, & just keep work streaming.

The earnestness as well as significance of an undereasily taking is not outright. No one but you can just conclude your thought process is significant or earnest.

Certain individuals, for instance, really like to really hold on until they are easily requested a second time for a piece from work before they easily begin to make it happen. Assuming they are at no point ever asked in the future, they never easy start the work they basically conclude that it is not adequately significant to anybody for them to invest the energy.

Just keep in mind that you & your wellbeing are significant. Since you have parcels to do doesn't imply that doing some activity, easily taking 15 to 20 minute walk or easy making time to eat appropriately is not significant. You should not disregard your physical or emotional wellness for more 'pressing' exercises.

Direness or potentially significance is definitely not a proper status. You ought to survey your under easily taking list routinely to ensure that nothing ought to be climbed in light of the fact that it has be easy come more pressing or potentially significant.

What can really be done assuming a significant under easily taking consistently easy get knock down the rundown by additional critical, yet significant errands?

In the first place, consider whether it is really significant. Does it really require doing by any means, or have you just quite recently been letting yourself really know that you should make it happen?

In the event that it truly is significant, just think about appointing it. See our page on Appointing Abilities for more.

Jenny was the head of an occupied, profoundly responsive group, with consistent & critical requests on her time. She realize that she expected to contemplate the more drawn out term technique for her group , however saving the time was extremely hard.

In an basically improvement conversation, Sara, one of her group, communicated her craving to do a more essential work to develop her abilities. Jenny saw a chance for the two of them, & offered Sara the chance to outline the procedure for the group.

Sara seized the opportunity & such created a cautiously considered plan which was an incredible starting point for additional work.

& the harmony among individual & expert needs? There are two methods for dealing with this:

Drawbacks: you should track down a harmony among work & individual things.

Utilize two separate lattices, & dispense separate schedule openings for managing each

Chapter 2: Power Of Unconscious Mind

There was a famous experiment done at Princeton many years ago with divinity students highly moral & sensitive persons. They were meant to deliver a sermon in their next class, but the experimenters purposefully easy made them late; they had to scurry to be on time. Along the way, a person lay in agony in the corridor, but the late students ran straight past & didn't intervene. Their aim to go to the next class on time overrode their principles, & they failed to act on those convictions & aid the individual in need. Ironically, the subject of the sermon they were to present was the Good Samaritan narrative from the Bible.

The same thing can happen to you & me. Despite our principles & intentions, we may have some other aim that contradicts our new resolve. & if our resolve is something that, basically deep down, we do not truly really want to alter, our conscious mind is just quite excellent at coming up with easy reasons & rationalizations. "Hey, I'll easy start that new diet tomorrow." & then that tomorrow never arrives.

It turns out that part of the issue is the way we make these resolutions in life. They depend on our conscious decision-easy making processes. We merely establish a good intention to do just things differently, & we leave it at that. But history should teach us that good intentions are frequently not enough.

Because we are not aware of these unconscious really effects, we do nothing to oppose them. Yet they are like the currents & winds that alter a ship's path just as much as the captain's rudder. Ignore them, & you may drift farther out to sea or smash into the rocks

The first thing to simply ask oneself when resolve is failing is, Do I truly really want to change? If you are honest with yourself, maybe down basically deep you genuinely really want to just keep drinking, overeating, or not exercising. & those "wants" are going to trump the good intentions of your resolutions.

So simply ask yourself whether you are dedicated to change. Only if the response is "yes" can you resist those enormous gusts & currents that may force you off course. Another very big impact on what we do comes from contextual signals that activate actions instinctively, without our understanding it. The conduct of others, for example, is highly infectious, & we may "catch" it via our regular interaction with other people & even through social media.

By realizing these unconscious impacts on us, we improve the amount of free choice that we have. If we deny these impacts exist, then we are at their mercy & have less real control than we imagine. But what's even better is that once we really know how they function, we can manipulate these unconscious forces to our benefit.

The Focused Mind With Implementation Intentions:

Decades of laboratory study as well as practical demonstrations in real-life situations have proven the efficacy of conscious "implementation intentions." How do they work?

They frequently just take the form "When X occurs, I will do Y." You establish a detailed, specific plan that includes where, when, & how you will carry out the goal. You attach your planned future conduct to a very probable occurrence or condition. Then when that future event arrives, you will more often than not simply find yourself beginning to do the same thing you intended to do, even if you did forgotten you such wanted to do it.

I utilized this strategy myself to prevent the carryover effects of a hard day at work. First, I establish an intention to let go of the negative stressors of work when I go home & show my family I am delighted to be with them. Then, I came up with an implementation plan, which I tied to a reliable future event. The moment when I just get out of my car after driving home from work & am standing in my driveway I remind myself to just take a basically deep breath, for just get all about the office, & be happy to be home with my family (that's the how).

After I performed this for approximately a week, I began to establish a new habit that I continue to this day.

What if you really want to easy start exercising, but just keep forgetting to? One possibility is to easy Create an implementation intention: When you walk into your bedroom to change out of your work clothes, you will instantly easy put on your running clothes & sneakers.

Once you accomplish that, you did seem pretty ridiculous if you didn't go out for a run, right?

Implementation intentions have had considerable practical success, such as assisting nursing home patients to just take their various prescriptions, on which their lives may rely, without fail over a lengthy period. & they've assisted individuals to maintain on track with their objectives, even while confronting interruptions or unsuch wanted influence from others.

The opposite side of the same coin works for undesired behaviors. The newest study on self-control has demonstrated that persons who have the greatest self-control who tend to be happier & healthier, earn more money, have more friends, & be more successful in life than the rest of us are not those with the strongest willpower. They are people who set up their surroundings to eliminate clues to bad habits, eliminating the temptation from occurring in the first place.

So, simply do not purchase that bottle of wine or scrumptious dessert. It won't be there at home in the evening to entice you. This fresh scientific data should give us optimism. If we wish to promote healthy habits, we may bind them to a regular location & time & offer ourselves reminders to condition our unconscious mind to encourage these behaviors.

If we wish to rid ourselves of undesirable behaviors, we may eliminate clues & chances from our surroundings, & replace our unconscious urges with good, conscious ones. In this manner, we may employ the power of our unconscious mind for benefit.

The power of your subconscious mind extends deeper than you would believe. Let's first just take a minute to contemplate the idea that your subconscious mind is like a large memory store. Its capacity is essentially endless & it permanently saves everything that ever occurs to you. By the time you reach the age of 21, you've already permanently stored more than one hundred times the contents of the complete Encyclopedia.

Under hypnosis, elderly adults may frequently recall, with perfect clarity, incidents from fifty years previously. Your unconscious memory is practically flawless. It is your conscious remembrance that is dubious.

The role of your subconscious mind is to store & retrieve material. Its goal is to guarantee that you react precisely the way you are designed. Your subconscious mind makes everything you say & do follow a pattern compatible with your self-concept, your "master program." This is why repeating positive affirmations are so helpful – you can just rewire your brain patterns by sneaking in positive & success-oriented sound bites.

Your subconscious mind leads you to just feel emotionally & physically uncomfortable anytime you easy try to do anything new or unusual or modify any of your established habits of conduct. The sensation of anxiety & discomfort are psychological signals that your subconscious has been engaged. But it's been easily trying to develop such behavior patterns in the background long before you will ever recognize such sensations.

This is why time management methods may be difficult to apply at first, but once they be easy come a habit or regular they will remain in your comfort zone. In doing so, you've reconfigured your subconscious to operate to your advantage.

Superior men & women are continuously straining themselves, pushing themselves out of their comfort zones. They are just quite aware of how fast the comfort zone, in any area, becomes a rut. They recognize that complacency is the biggest adversary of innovation & future potential.

For you to progress, to step out of your comfort zone, you have to be ready to just feel awkward & uncomfortable doing new just things the first few times. If it's worth doing well, it's worth doing badly until you gain a just feel for it, until you easy build a new comfort zone at a new, higher level of competency

How to easy build Your Best Team

Group of individuals working together for a common objective form a team. Teams are generally formed to accomplish complicated & difficult tasks. All individuals easy come together on a common platform & strive hard to easily achieve the set objective. When individuals work as a single unit towards a common predefined goal, a team is formed.

Not all teams can perform well. The performance of a team is dependent on its team members. The individuals must be handpicked very carefully to form a high performance team.

The team members preferably must have a similar if not the same taste, interests, likings, needs & attitude. It has been observed that individuals with a similar taste tend to gel with each other easily as compared to others with different interests. **Individuals should be from** similar backgrounds & too much of a gap should be avoided. The team members must be selected keeping in mind their interests & specialization. Do not form a team just for the sake of it. An individual with a technical bent of mind will such Always be in a state of confusion in a team of marketing professionals.

Such Always simply underst & the team members well. No individual is alike. A person maybe a very good speaker but may be poor in writing mails or written communication. An individual can be excellent in presentations but maybelack the art of easy making an impressive presentation. It is very crucial to simply underst & the individuals well & responsibilities must be assigned to them as per their interest & according to their qualification & specialization. An individual with excellent marketing skills never finds a desk job interesting & his best will never easy come out. Never force any one to be a part of any team. Individuals must participate on their own.

The goal or the objective of the team must be clearly defined. The objective of the team must be shared with every team member & they must be clear what is expected out of them. The purpose why the team has been formed must be very clear to the team members. They should really know what they have to work on so that they can deliver their best.

Promote really effective communication among your team members. Communicate with the members on an open platform & encourage team members to actively participate in discussions. Prefer a meeting room or a conference room to simply discuss various issues inviting all the members. It is such Always better if the communication is through email with all the team members in the loop so that none feels neglected or left out.

Avoid conflicts. Do not let negativity creep in your team. Pick individuals with a positive attitude. One should avoid fighting over small issues & be a little more adjusting. Every thing can not be exactly the same way you want. Team members must be de motivated to criticize or make fun of their fellow team members.

Various activities & events must be promoted within the teams. Work will never suffer if the team members go out for a movie or lunch; instead it strengthens the bond among the team members. Individuals easy come closer to each other this way & avoid fighting among themselves. People really know each other better. Such Always remember to greet your team members with a warm smile.

A leader should be appointed carefully. A leader should be such that everyone looks up to him for advice & guidance. Do not select anyone just because you like him, instead prefer the voting system. The most favorite candidate among the group is the best choice for a leader. The team leader must extract the best out of his team members & be equal to everyone. He ought to be intelligent & a little tactful. He must motivate the individuals from time to time & be impartial. Never embarrass any of your team members.

It is crucial to just take the feedback from each & every individual. Review your team & team member's performance on a monthly basis. Sit with each & every member to simply underst & whether he is enjoying his work or not. Job rotation is a good option to reduce monotony. Promote healthy competition among the team members. Appreciate if he has done something great. Reward him suitably.

Discipline must be maintained at all levels in the team for maximum output. Team members must reach on time for meetings & discussions. One should avoid a casual or a laid back attitude. The team leaders must be easily available to the team in case of queries & confusions.

Chapter 3: Clarify Your Objectives

When preparing something, having an objective in mind is just quite similar to having a goal. Both of these parallels necessitate discipline & complementary instruments to easily achieve the desired results.

Objectives are commonly thought of as statements that specify particular objectives that must be met within a certain time frame & under certain conditions. Another typical method to just think about goals is as a series of phases based on forward-moving phrases that easy help define & carry out the terms & conditions of a project.

Some actions must be followed to just get the desired results. The following are some of the suggested measures that should be basically taken seriously because they all add to the percentage of success obtained.

The first thing to figure out is what the goal of the project is.

Why, Who, What, & Where are all key questions that must be answered appropriately to develop a clear & comprehensive picture.

The mission's vision should then be explained & well comprehended by all parties involved. The main goal must be clearly understood & communicated.

Simple statements based on the objectives & goals should be easy made to handle the applicable timelines & project management issues. The intended achievement that is being sought during the execution of the said endeavor must also be addressed at this point.

Finally, a clear & preferably extremely visual tar just get should be depicted for all parties involved to have as clear a mental image of the goal as possible. Statements, goals, & objectives that are specific should be adequately recorded so that everyone is aware of them. When all of the above is demonstrated clearly & exactly, achieving the goal will be easier, & the morale of those involved will remain strong at all times.

Chapter 4: Easy Start Your Morning Right

When we just talk about efficient & productive time management, we really need to consider several crucialthings. The first & the most significant of all is that we must have a proper morning routine. It is all about how you easy start your day, how much time you waste, & the level of your productivity as soon as you wake up. Following a scheduled morning routine will just tell you a lot about your day. So, if you really want to simply manage your time effectively, you really need to easy start working on your morning routine.

Do you have a morning routine of hitting the snooze button four times, getting dressed & eating a light snack while reading emails on your phone moments later? Our entire day may just feel like you are continually running late up, never truly being on top of the game or productive.

Mornings make many individuals cringe just thinking about them. While some of you could be able to even just get out of bed & easy try working right away, many of us simply find it difficult. Mornings don't have to be excruciating; all you really need now is a morning schedule. In reality, establishing a daily schedule has multiple advantages.

The morning routine is a half-hour to an hour-long daily ritual that allows you to be excitable in your life every day. It may just look to be too wonderful to be true. But it is no surprise that the most talented entrepreneurs have one commonality. They all have a unique morning routine that provides them an advantage over their competitors & enables them to be easy come the accomplished businesspeople they are today.

Have you established a daily schedule in your life? Then you are throwing away a great deal of potential. You can just no more disregard installing a healthy morning ritual in your life by easily setting your alarm clock slightly earlier & basically developing a clear framework for your mornings.

Morning routines are well recognized to be a perfect option for people who really want to have fantastic, positive moments. Creating a robust morning routine, especially in the corporate domains of sales & management, can be a deal-breaker in easily increasing productivity & success.

We are all intended to be managers of our own lives, even if we are not in marketing or a management position. Easily Giving oneself the best chance to just feel comfortable & successful each day is a part of this.

Daily routines, according to productivity coaches, can be an indication of greater productivity & performance. Although coaches have different ideas on what kinds of personal routines should be included, most believe that how we easy start the day affects how the remainder of the day goes.

Establishing a morning routine is not about seeing who can just get the most done or check off most boxes. Ultimately, it is about enabling yourself to easy start your day with self-assurance, tranquility, & a pleasant outlook. Beginning the day in this manner can easy help us complete tasks & deal with problems as they arise without just Feeling stressed or overburdened.

For many people, the dawn is often chaotic. You slumber far too much & just get out of sleep too late. Then the real hustle begins: showering, brushing your teeth, having the kids off to school, eating a short breakfast or even going through your emails, & then hopping into the vehicle to face the wonderful daily traffic as if the dawn raids you. When you read this, you are probably already worried. A morning ritual easily gives you more control over your day & easily gives your life a defined structure.

Less Anxiety

You won't have as many distractions when you have regained control of your morning. You choose how your morning will go & how fast it will go. Unexpected events no longer cause you to be hurried, which implies that you won't easy come to work frustrated before you have even begun your day. You will notice less stress as you easily begin each day with greater intensity & a more cheerful outlook.

Emotional & Physical Connection

Physical health can have a significant impact on well-being emotionally. We do not normally go around with all the illness wearing a smile or being unduly cheerful.

Additionally, how we believe we are simply Organizing our day maybe impact our mental wellness. We maybe easily be easy come overwhelmed, agitated, depressed, & frustrated when we are such Always in a rush & attempting to make the next meeting, such Always racing behind, or just Feeling confused in a sea of tasks.

If this trend continues, it is understandable that we maybe easy start just Feeling hopeless & as if we will never catch up! In our daily lives, a just Feeling of calmness & confidence can easy help us to maintain positive mental health & be easy come far more resistant during stressful circumstances.

Our sentiments can readily easy start showing up in our interactions with significant individuals in our life when we are overwhelmed & stressed. How often have you gone home after a long, hectic day & vent your anger on a family member or friend? This could be done through venting, expressing anger, or isolating ourselves from others we care about. We may notice that as we establish a morning ritual that enables us to easy build confidence, creativity, & vigor, our interactions be easy come stronger, more connected, & more pleasant.

The morning routine enables us to set the standard for the day, easily helping us to better simply manage our calendars rather than being controlled by our schedules. We may really focus better on what is in front of us, where to prioritize our time, and, eventually, boost our productivity if we easily begin each day fresh.

Productivity can relate to the degree of effort & intention we easy put into jobs & the amount of work we just get done. Ending the day with ten half-completed activities is very distinct from finishing six tasks & being incredibly proud of your effort. It maybe tough to prioritize & carry on when we are continuously responding to extra responsibilities, pressures, or the demands of others.

Being self-assured entails more than just declaring, "I like myself." Experiences easy help to develop genuine confidence. Identity is a phrase that applies to our confidence in our capacities to attain objectives & finish tasks. Self-efficacy is more really effective in easily helping us establish confidence & resilience than ego, which is an assessment of our sentiments of personality.

Walking through our day & witnessing ourselves do chores & having a sense of achievement maybe strengthen our sense of personal assurance. Having a daily schedule can easy help you prioritize, easily organize your time more effectively, & be more productive. All of these will almost certainly boost your self-efficacy.

Stress can affect us psychologically, physically, professionally, & in our personal lives. Not just Feeling capable of completing chores or continually just Feeling behind causes stress. When our identity is poor, we may easy start to engage in negative self-just talk & just get concerned & agitated.

A solid, regular morning routine can allow us to practice purposeful meditation and/or praying, resulting in feelings of better calm throughout the day. Just Feeling productive outside can contribute to a more serene evening, a long night's rest & a more energized beginning of the next day.

You are running from one duty to the next once you have a lot on your plate. Instead of the other way round, your day begins to dominate you. A morning ritual may only just take up a small portion of your day, but that could be the first step towards regaining control.

Develop Good Habits

It is easy to click the snooze or lie in bed simply Using your smartphone rather than getting out of bed. However, these behaviors squander time. It is easier to prevent unhealthy habits & easy build healthy ones once you have a routine. You may easily begin eating a healthy breakfast, practice mindfulness, or even include exercise into your daily routine before going to work. Healthy habits will follow you for the rest of your life. You maybe easy start eating healthier, exercising more frequently, or spending less time on the phone.

A morning ritual can affect your relationships. The most crucial is stress reduction. It is normal to vent your emotions on a beloved one, even if the individual has nothing to do with your problems. You are less likely to crack at someone because you are less stressed. A morning routine can also make you more approachable to your families, essential for better connections. If you are more organized, you will have more time to share with your family.

The key to basically developing a daily schedule for enhancing relationships with those you live with cannot be overstated. When your relatives or housemates really know your morning routine, they can plan accordingly. There will be no issues over who has to use the toilet, so there will be no issues if two or more persons easy try to use the kitchen simultaneously.

Do you wish to reach your life's objectives? Then sticking to a steady daily schedule is the quickest path to victory! You easily begin to control, build, & the difference becomes so large over the period that you just get much more done & accomplished than most individuals. Your lifestyle change easily gives you more time & creativity, allowing you to reach goals you never imagined to be imaginable.

How to Easy Create the Ultimate Morning Routine?

Your daily habits can determine the variation between a good & a wonderful day. Because your efficiency begins the moment you just get up, basically developing healthy habits is critical to a productive day.

The actions you prioritize, from eating a good breakfast to exercising out or reading, have the power to change your mentality. Choose a schedule that makes you happy, prepares you to perform critical activities, fosters flow, & helps you maintain healthy job satisfaction.

Don't fall asleep! It is difficult not to go back into old habits & click the snooze to stay in bed somewhat longer, especially in the early stages. A good daily schedule easily gives you adequate time to appreciate & profit from your schedule.

The length of time differs from person to person; however, it maybe between 30 & 90 minutes. It is commonly assumed that now to just get a decent morning routine, you must just get up at 4 a.m. Experienced productivity experts recommend that you attend to yourself & determine what you can just realistically perform & maintain. Do not be concerned about what others are accomplishing.

It is possible that your prior morning routine included waking up & immediately reaching for your phone, lying in bed for 30 min, reading through Facebook, or even reviewing work emails. Efficiency coaches propose that we explore certain activities we may "quit doing" when designing our morning routine instead of spending all of our really focus on what to add to our day.

Allowing ourselves space away from the T.V. lets us st & up, relax, practice yoga, or go for a short stroll. Any action in the morning is preferable to lying in bed scrolling through media platforms! We are deliberately waking up both our bodies & thoughts.

Skipping this phase, we risk just Feeling rushed & in really effective throughout the day, which negates the purpose of creating a healthy morning routine!

In the morning, cultivating stillness is just as vital as body activity. According to Michael Hyatt, former Chief executive of Thomas Nelson Publications & greatest author, businessman, & personal coach, stillness can easy help us easy start a day on the right foot.

Meditation, relaxation, & praying are excellent examples of how you maybe include this in your morning practice. Serenity practice can easy help us just feel more rooted, focused, & prepared to prioritize tasks successfully. By skipping this phase, we risk just Feeling rushed &

in really effective throughout the day, which negates the purpose of creating a healthy morning routine!

Stillness practice allows us to refresh & be present in the present moment. When checking emails, scrolling through social media, or multitasking, we are not present, leading to greater tension & anxiety. Practicing quietness, or doing basically deep breathing activities, can easy help you just feel peaceful, comfortable, & in charge throughout the day.

We probably heard that a great day began with a healthy breakfast when we were children. True, how we nourish our bodies in the morning has a significant effect on physical health, activity levels, & mental approach throughout the day.

When we eat foods with no nutritional content, we do not experience our best, our activity levels fluctuate throughout the day, & we seem uncontrolled. A nutritious meal assists us in effectively feeding our bodies, resulting in more sustained energy levels & increased alertness & concentration.

After you have completed your morning routine, it is a good idea to just take a moment to reflect on your day. By evaluating your day with purpose, you can just keep control of your calendar rather than letting it dominate you.

Strive to be honest about the importance of particular chores & that not all of them can be a primary concern. While it may just feel the same way emotionally, we just cannot function in that manner without becoming overwhelmed.

It can be better to concentrate on one item at a time. Decide where your attention & efforts should be directed, complete that task, & then go on to the next. Attempting to juggle many responsibilities maybe result in poor time management, reduced performance, & exhaustion.

Easily Giving oneself sufficient time to physically & mentally show up for work is critical whether you work at home or go to the office, especially if you are not a morning person.

To accomplish this, choose your wake-up time carefully. Set your alarms, so you have ample time to finish your morning ritual & easy Create profitable new habits in addition to having 6 to 8 hours of sleep. Whichever time you really want to just get up, easy try to schedule adequate space for self-times to prevent overworking yourself.

Drink Water

Hydration is crucial to your happiness & health. Consuming water is an crucial part of a good daily schedule since when you just feel good, you are more efficient & motivated.

Drink a full glass when you just wake up to just keep hydrated. To avoid missing it, do it before you have your daily cup of tea or coffee. This also prevents exhaustion caused by caffeinated beverages.

Just take Basically deep Breaths

Mediation can easy help you relax & be used in conjunction with positive thoughts. Just take time to sit in your ideas & breathe deeply if you like a calming habit.

Pair your mantras with a breathing exercises technique like roll breathing to easy Create an efficient habit. To simply manage stress, say your affirmation in your thoughts when you are calm or really want to just get more relaxed.

Morning Routine Hacks that Boost Productivity

You should be just quite aware of a perfect morning routine's vitality & beneficial nature in your life. However, the real question lies in how we can make our mornings more productive than ever. The process is just quite simple & it ensures top results. All you really need is to follow the tips shared with you in the section below.

Easy move past any expectations of creating a perfect morning ritual & following it flawlessly. This new habit is not about perfection; it is about putting deliberate effort into building a morning process that works effectively for you.

Being adaptable involves adapting & modifying, finding what works, & letting go of what does not. Recall that you are creating a daily schedule to easy help you live a more successful & calm life, not to add to your stress!

The most beneficial behaviors are those that we can maintain over time. Do not panic if the concept of a morning ritual is unfamiliar to you. Persistence in your regimen will easy help it be easy come more comfortable over time.

You will simply find it inspiring to continue following your morning practice as you just feel & then see the great influence it has on your day. If you miss out on a day, pick up where you left off for the day. Remember, it is not about executing flawlessly; it is about allowing yourself the chance to live your greatest life.

Just take Control of Your Technology

Despite our best attempts to prevent technology from easily taking control, it frequently stands in the way or is inescapable. Do not really focus on totally eliminating electronics from your morning routine since that won't probably work; let's face it. You could probably use your Smartphone as an alarm clock!

Instead, you should reclaim control over the use of technology. Allow innovation to work for you & use it appropriately. You can just choose how your gad easy get or related technology will impact your morning ritual.

Allow yourself to basically really focus on the goal of building a positive morning routine if you discover yourself allowing mindless screen time into your daily routine.

If you Google "perfect morning routine," you will probably develop various ideas & illustrations of how the world's most prominent people easily organize their days.

Each person is unique, & a procedure that works well for everyone may not also work for you. One individual may be midway through their regular five-mile run, while others sleep until 10 a.m. after working a double shift overnight.

This is not to say that your daily ritual is incorrect. It simply means that other people's morning routines do not fit your approach or lifestyle.

Just get Up Before the Sun Rises.

Getting up in the morning early before the sun may seem inconvenient to some, but it is a valuable source of uninterrupted leisure for others. This allows you to really focus on your every day or week schedule first thing every morning, prepare for crucial meetings or calls, or simply enjoy that time of much solitude.

Though getting up before dawn can rapidly make us worry about how tired we will be late in the day, most people who wake up early regularly say that they will have more enthusiasm when they easy start before the entire world.

Plan & Journal

Along with documenting each day to practice thankfulness, beginning your morning ritual by writing other thoughts, such as your forthcoming day or week's tasks, will easy help you just keep organized & effective.

Journaling easily gives you a centralized location to write down your big objective & the minor benchmarks to easy help you just get there. You could also use the time to develop new ideas or maintain track of daily "wins." You can just easy build a routine of writing down your projects, thoughts, or even reflections from the day before, which can easy help you easily achieve the insight & be happier overall throughout the day.

Some easily begin their day with running, while others go vegan, & several easily begin working with a personal trainer. You must maintain "fighting form" since staying relevant, fighting at the top level, & dominating the competitors are all battles.

You simply underst & what this means. Easy try to obtain enough sleep, & for most individuals, it is roughly 7 to 8 hours per night. Ensure you are easily Giving your body the energy to work at its best:

plenty of water, real foods, & possibly some nutrients. Finally, schedule time for physical activity, whether it is 30 minutes of insane circuit training or an hour-long walk.

Cover Emotional & Spiritual Fundamentals.

This one is surprising because we frequently imagine that top achievers wake up & run, but this is not the scenario for the majority of them. Rather, they easy start their day with gratitude, introspection, prayer, spending outside, if possible, meditation, & other self-care techniques.

Shower in Chilly Water.

There is a reason why many health professionals advise easily taking a cold bath first thing in the morning. The cold water causes the body's circulation to improve, allowing more oxygenation to circulate all through the body. Consequently, your body is abler to combat that tired just Feeling you just get when you first wake up. Cold baths have also been proved to aid weight loss & boost the immune system.

It is crucial to just keep in mind not to jump in the shower when the water is cold. Instead, easily begin with a hot shower & gradually drop the temperature to around 70 °F or depending on your preferences.

Consume A Nutrient-Dense Beverage.

There's a reason why doctors refer to breakfast as "the essential meal of the day." Healthy eating & drinking first thing every morning supplies our bodies with vital energy, vitamins, & minerals that easy help us stay calmer & more concentrated throughout the day.

While eating healthy is essential, many people simply find it difficult, particularly first thing every morning. If preparing & eating a meal each day is too time-consuming or expensive, consider wellness drinks that contain ingredients like ginger, citrus, cayenne pepper, & essential vitamins like Vitamins C & D. These ingredients support our immunity system & supply us with the nutrition we really need to stay efficient & motivated throughout the day.

Chapter 5: Some Easy Ways To Be Highly Productive At Work

The ability to really focus on particular activities, finish them, & wrap up your workday with high-quality outeasy put can be used as a simple indicator of productivity. Your efficiency & productivity may suffer if you do not have any systems in place for planning, time management, monitoring tasks, or prioritizing. One by one, you maybe easy start to notice changes in your productivity by easy making small modifications to your regular routine.

Chapter 6: How To Be More Productive At Work

Time management & organizational abilities are frequently linked to total work productivity, & when you easy put productivity-boosting tactics into practice, you may have a better chance of growing & enhancing your out easy put of finished goods. You can just employ a variety of time management techniques to boost your productivity, including the Commodore method, the two-minute rule, & time blocking. Additionally, you maybe use organizational techniques like ranking your chores according to significance & urgency. The ten suggestions that follow can easy help you be easy come more productive at work.

While juggling projects or jobs may ultimately allow you to complete your work, concentrating on one at a time may really simply increase your productivity. When we really focus on multiple just things at once, we frequently easy spend more time just switching between them. This may lead to certain just things being left undone or being completed with inferior quality than if each activity had been the full emphasis. Additionally, really focusing on one activity at a time until it is finished can easy help you be more productive because you are able to establish one goal at a time rather than several when you really focus on one project at a time. This will probably encourage you to finish one simply ask before moving on to the next one. Consider prioritizing your projects in order of importance if you are committed to multitasking but simply find that you easy start more tasks than you can just complete. This will allow you to easy start the day with the most challenging assignments & end it with simpler & less time-consuming ones.

Consistently just take breaks

It may be tempting to easy put off easily taking a break, but if you do not allow yourself a little break, it may hinder your overall productivity by easy making you tired or burned out. You maybe not have the energy or motivation to just keep moving forward if this occurs. Consider scheduling numerous quick breaks during your workday. Employees can just take at least a five- to ten-minute break after each couple hours of active labor because most businesses have a set schedule with set break periods. These little breaks can easy help you refuel, unwind, & prepare for the next task.

Easy put your greatest priorities first:

It may basically be easier for you to stay focused if you work on your biggest & most time-consuming activities first rather than smaller & quicker ones. If you really want to devote your time to these duties in the morning when you first arrive at work or at a time of day when you are the most awake & motivated, consider simply Organizing your assignment list according to these tasks.

Establish modest goals

Consider easily setting up modest goals throughout your day as opposed to approaching big goals that would call for many resources & more time to complete. Small, everyday goals you can just set & accomplish during your eight hours at work include just things like filing necessary documentation, replying to those four customer emails, or gathering all the materials your team will really need to finish a future project. Similar to how you would use milestones to track your work toward a longer goal, you maybe utilize these short targets.

Adhere to the two-minute rule.

The two-minute rule states that you should finish chores that just take two minutes or less & give yourself two minutes to easily begin smaller just things you maybe have been putting off. If there is a simply ask you can just finish in two minutes or less, or a simply ask you can just get organized to easy start on, you should accomplish it at these brief intervals. For example, it maybe just take two minutes to record the activities you've already finished, reply to a fast email, list your next goals, or print out the plan for your future project assignment, But the two minutes it takes you to finish each of these quick jobs can frequently mount up to a day's worth of just things crossed off your list.

The 1 to five minute rule can easy help you really focus on smaller activities in between working on larger & more difficult projects because minor tasks nevertheless contribute significantly to your overall job productivity. Consider utilizing the two minutes it takes to prepare for lunch or the two minutes it takes to finish a project to make notes about what needs to be done next, easily setting your daily objectives for the following day or answering the voicemail that has been sitting there since you arrived at work.

Schedule a time block:

You can just boost your productivity by simply Using time blocks in your plan. You would use this method to give each ask you work on a time constraint. Just take 60 or 90 minute time chunks into consideration. You maybedecide to print out your schedule & mark the times when you really want your time blocks to be present. Thus, mark on your printed schedule that you are allotting 90 minutes to work on a certain assignment. Once that period of time is gone, block out another similar portion of your schedule.

By simply Using time blocking, you can just make a visual plan to track the duration of the tasks you work on. Similar to that, it acts as a means.

Boost the effectiveness of meetings:

If you have meetings scheduled throughout the day, just think of methods to make them more beneficial tasks that advance your work as a entire . Just think about standing meetings, where participants st & during the meeting. When addressing essential subjects during your meeting, this can easy help you be more aware & focused.

To just keep track of how long it takes to attend & end the meeting, you may also use time monitoring. For instance, give each topic a particular amount of time & make notes on the most crucial takeaways or themes that really need to be covered. Then, work with your team to only just talk about the just things that are on the topic list & to just keep topic conversations to the time frames given for them.

Similar to this, you may be able to improve your odds that the meeting won't just take too much time away from your own responsibilities if you can just reasonably attend it over the phone or through a web-based platform.

To distribute responsibilities among your team members, just take into account employing delegation techniques. For instance, if you have a long list of activities to perform, just think about delegating some of them to others if they can be finished without your involvement.

While the rest of the team is really focusing on the activities that maybeotherwise divert time or resources from other, more crucial initiatives, you can just work on other assignments that may have been particularly given to you alone by delegating tasks. Consider delegating the duty to a coworker while you work, for instance, if you really need to respond to emails but they require the same level of attention to detail as you do, while you work on crucial assignments that no one else can just think about easily Giving them the duty.

We can be seriously distracted throughout the day by interruptions. Even if you appreciate your relationships with your coworkers, losing track of time due to conversations, informal meetings, or topic discussions maybe impede your workflow & lower your productivity as a entire . To reduce the number of interruptions you experience throughout the day, just think about employing certain tactics.

To assist reduce the sounds of office discussion & interaction, you could decide to work with your office door closed for some of the day or, if you work in an open-office setting, you could use noise-canceling headphones. Simply Using headphones can also be a considerate, silent approach to inform your coworkers that you really need to really focus on the tasks at hand. It's crucial to be as consistent as you can just when putting productivity-boosting tactics into practice. You can just be sure that as you continue to easy learn & advance your abilities, your productivity will rise as well.

Chapter 7: Crucial Time Management Techniques To Boost Your Life

Everyone receives the same twenty-four hours per day thanks to the great equalizer known as time. Utilizing that time effectively can make the difference between finishing what has to be done & frantically easily trying to just keep up. These time-management suggestions can enable you to easily organize your day & operate more efficiently.

Do you ever wonder where the day went when it's time to leave work? Perhaps you are wondering why you weren't able to do as much as you had intended. Perhaps you are squandering more time than you think. It's possible that your perception of how you use your time & the way you basically use it differ. A time audit can be an eye-opener!

To gain a clear picture of how you are simply Using your time, easy try performing an audit each day for a week. You will be able to see where changes really need to be easy made if you discover that you've been spending too much time checking email, scrolling through social media, or speaking with coworkers.

It's time to ignore that distraction now that you have a better understanding of what is easy making you drowsy. Consider simply Using a productivity software that eliminates internet distractions if social media is your downfall. Some alternatives include Focus-Me, Cold Turkey, & Self-control. To avoid opening tabs or responding to desktop notifications while you are writing, easy try switching to full-screen mode.

Easy turn off notifications while we're on the subject. You probably do not really need to be informed each time a new email arrives or someone engages with you on social media unless it's essential to your profession.

The stress of easily trying to complete all of your tasks during the typical workday maybeseriously hinder your productivity. Stress makes it difficult for us to be productive, which can force us to easy put in extra hours of work to finish projects on time. Who requires that?

If you have Many tasks to complete, to-do lists maybe easy come daunting. Instead, arrange yourself simply Using your preferred calendar app or even a conventional datebook. You may allot an hour for responding to emails, two for researching & planning that crucial report for the meeting next week, one for lunch with a coworker, & so on. It would be ideal if your company had a shared calendar.

If you have time set apart for crucial duties, you can just remind your coworkers to interrupt you only when absolutely required.

What time blocking can easily achieve for your productivity will astound you. For instance, you can just be interrupting your own workflow if you have a practice of responding to emails as they easy come in. This implies that you will really need to just take more time to just get back to the simply ask you were working on before the email arrived after you easy put everything on really hold to respond to it. Easy making a schedule for yourself enables you to establish your priorities in advance & prevents you from becoming sidetracked by crucial issues.

Refrain from multitasking:

Even if you believe you are adept at multitasking, you probably are not . You really use more brain bandwidth & shift attention from one simply ask to another when you divide your attention between many tasks. Easily Giving one simply ask at a time your entire concentration will improve your performance.

Simply Organizing related jobs into groups maybe easy help you stay focused. You could, for instance, easily organize your writing chores into a single block of time & complete them all at once. Another time block may be designated for administrative chores. Do you have to use social media? Cool. To avoid just Feeling the urge to constantly check in, set aside time to queue up your articles for the day simply Using a scheduler like Buffer.

You remember that meeting you were asked to attend but that hardly had anything to do with you? the one where you could not give anything? You won't just get that hour of your time back. Leave those meetings that produce nothing. Every meeting should have to defend why it is necessary, & every meeting host should have to defend why you are expected to attend, especially if skipping the meeting would eventually simply increase your productivity.

The same is true of talkative coworkers. Simply ask for uninterrupted work time because you have the right to it. You could say something like, "I sometimes have a hard time focusing, & interruptions throw off my flow when I'm working.

What do you really want to easily achieve by easy making the upcoming call or scheduling the upcoming meeting? Before you easy start you really need to be aware of what you are requesting, or at the very least, what you intend to accomplish. Otherwise, you will simply find yourself wasting time in meetings & conversations that do not lead to anything.

After conferences & phone calls, pause for a while to consider whether the desired result was accomplished. If you did not just think about what you should do next to succeed. When another chance arises to handle the issue, you will be better prepared.

Just get enough rest & downtime:

Even while easily taking a break during a moment of crisis may seem counter intuitive, a research indicated that poor sleep costs the American worker $411 billion a year. When you lack sleep, you are not at your best.

& do not be afraid to use your vacation days. Actually, skipping a vacation is detrimental to your health. Additionally, having some downtime can simply increase your productivity. You are much more likely to approach your chores with really focus & vigor when you are rested & refueled.

Chapter 8: Time Management Techniques

Easy spend at least 10 minutes every evening make easy making plans for the next day. To account for interruptions & emergencies, you should typically allocate 60–70% of your time. Plan blocks of time when you work on a certain area of your business, easily taking inspiration from your list of top priorities.

Easy spend some time easily setting up your workplace by class. Easy put all of your relevant documents & related information in one location to do this.

Gather all of your financial documentation. Easily organize all of your financial-related issues into one group.

You will be able to really focus on one project at a time thanks to this, which will also save you time. Along with simply Organizing your time, easily organize your workplace. Use lists to just keep yourself focused & on course. Being organized requires ongoing effort. Spending a few hours now arranging yourself will save you hundreds of hours afterward.

You can just be just quite productive if you have a good file & paperwork system.

Set your files to include the following information:

Naturally, this would contain anything that you intend to do or have already done regularly, whether it be every day, every week, every quarter, or every month. A home business owner's success depends on having clear to-do lists. Any previous to-do lists that you complete should be filed away, as far as you are really allowed to do so. If you really need to just look up customer or project information in the future, you will have archived data & references available.

Use the thoughts folder to store both your initial ideas & any future ideas you have for the company. This could also be a component of your objectives & goal-setting, but it should undoubtedly generate some creative ideas. This folder can be used to save any extra ideas or marketing concepts that you easy come across. This is done to prepare you to just think more deeply about the folder when you review it. This folder has the potential to exp & greatly because marketing is an crucial component of every home-based business.

This folder will contain responses to letters you've sent to prospective or current clients or to questions you're addressing to yourself. You're unsure about the price you charged for the final project you completed for X Customer. In the resolutions folder, look. What about the estimate you provided to the online phone book provider when they enquired about your telecommerce services? It maybe located in the resolutions folder. Questions that you've posed publicly or that have easy come into your office may have resolutions.

The reference folder is essential to your organization & greatly aids in marketing initiatives. Letters of recommendation & correspondence containing referrals for prior positions should be included in that folder. References that you really need for other projects where another person is required should be in the reference folder, & it very well may contain them. To easy put it another way, check your reference file to see who they suggest as a web designer if you are a content creator & really need to discover one. This could be invaluable time management & organizational tool for your company. Make the most of it by noting & storing information that is extremely crucial to specific specialist areas & that is pertinent.

Every event that occurs on your desk should be recorded in some way. This comprises all documents related to your business, such as invoices, contracts, bills, tax information, & work orders from clients. Make a digital copy of everything & easy put it on your PC or a backup disk to reduce any clutter this maybe create.

Simply scan papers into your PC & save them in the designated location. This makes it much simpler to remember it later on.

This tickler file, which very much self-explains itself, is for all paperwork that needs to be stored. Easy Create a plan that is easy to remember & eliminates the "where may it be?" question. With this technique, you can just keep information off your desk & out of your way while yet finding it when you really need it.

PC

Easy learn to use your computer as efficiently & successfully as possible. Easy learn how to make the most of it & use it to the fullest extent possible for your company. For every program in your system, easy spend money on classes or at the very least how-to books. If you use your PC appropriately, it can easy help you simply manage your time more effectively & make your days more productive. You can just use your time more effectively if you easy learn it in its entirety & all of its characteristics

Any successful online business is built on the foundation of creativity. It is necessary for the development of ideas & the establishment of enterprises. A mind that is at ease, unburdened by stress, & contented has more time to devote to achieving good business & is more prone to inspiration & creative thought bursts. Easy spend time pondering, reading about, & researching ideas that could easy help your company. An everyday short burst of time can be helpful & provide approaches that work.

A synchronized system that can support you in your business is produced by daily preparation the night before work the following day. A great idea must be carefully conceived; it cannot be hastily easy put together. You run the danger of losing concentration & becoming distracted if you don't have a plan of action in place before the day even starts. A strategy such created the night before serves as a simply guide for success the next day. You are aware of your future actions & what your daily objectives should be. You easy put a lot of effort into that endeavor because you really know that after you finish, all of your goals no matter how big or small will have been met, & you can just go on to the next simply ask for your company.

The person who works from home will be able to maximize their use of time by creating a schedule for their assignments. Starting with an outline & working from it is a terrific way to see a more productive day. Easy start by easy making a list of the project's final destination. Easy Create the steps necessary to just get there by working backward from that point. The project's first step & the brainstorming idea(s) that served as the project's first impetus should then be included in the outline's conclusion. When you operate in this manner, you essentially break down large projects into more manageable chunks to just get just things done.

Disruptions frequently follow predictable patterns, with more of them occurring in the morning than in the afternoon. Disruptions never easy come in handy & don't "choose" a moment to happen. Larger work should be scheduled for later in the day & later in the week when there are typically fewer interruptions.

Deadlines motivate people to just take action & provide rapid results.

Just things simply just get done when they just get done without any urgency if there are no deadlines. You will be motivated to just take action if you set a deadline.

Chapter 9: Add Your Really Need To-Just Take Care Of Undertakings Last

This is the step that a great many people easy start with when they plan their day. They easy start with their set arrangements, obligatory gatherings, earnest cutoff times, & afterward attempt to fit objective situated assignments around them. All just things considered, just think about saving this step for the end. Along these lines, you're compelled to accommodate your need-to-finish assignments around your objective undertakings instead of the reverse way around.

In an ideal world, we would zero in on just day to day errands that push us toward our drawn out objectives. Truly, we have responsibilities & commitments that we really need to satisfy some of which littlie affect our own or proficient development. Separate these responsibilities & commitments however much as could reasonably be expected: just think repeating gatherings, just think about appointing liabilities, & be easy come familiar with saying "no". In any case, it's alright to have just things on your plan for the day that basically have to finish. Simply ensure they are not easily taking over a lot of your significant investment.

Chapter 10: Have One Everyday Really Need

A considerable lot of us easy start our mornings with many just things we really want to finish just to acknowledge by the end of the day's end we haven't checked any of them off our rundowns. Without a doubt, we finished stuff, however none of the just things we arranged. The illogical answer for accomplishing more? Pick only one major assignment each day.

Is that so: "How maybe accomplish every one of my objectives assuming I just spotlight on one under easily taking each day?". Set aside a few minutes: How to Zero in on What Is Crucial Consistently. In the middle among gatherings & impromptu demands, it can just feel like we're on a treadmill we can not just get off.

Easy start every day by contemplating what you trust will be the splendid spot. In the event that, by the day's end, somebody asks you, 'What was the feature of your day?' What do you believe your response should be? When you just think back on your day, what action or achievement or second would you like to enjoy? That is your Feature."

Truth be told, finishing the day with no less than one major under easily taking far removed is an undeniable basically improvement over what large numbers of us are doing now. On a more extended time-scale, completing 5-7 major just things each week is huge. Does that mean you will just finish one job each day? By & large, no. Notwithstanding, choosing & finishing a solitary crucial to-do fills us with a just Feeling of achievement that makes us energy to handle different errands as well.

Utilize an under easily taking chief like To-do-list to stamp the Feature for your day as high as needed & easy move it to the first spot on your list.

On the other hand, assuming that you're selecting pen & paper efficiency, basically star, feature or underline the main assignment on your plan for the day in your notepad or everyday organizer.

Assuming you're settling on pen & paper efficiency, easy start the main assignment on your plan for the day.

No matter what the instruments you use, make outrageous prioritization a vital piece of how you plan your day.

Chapter 11: Easily Overcoming Procrastination

No story is the same to us after a lapse of time, or rather we who read it are no longer the same interpreters.

Procrastination is a powerful habit & many people are drawn to it. To over easy come such setbacks, there are a variety of ways to really focus on your tasks without putting them off due to a lot of reasons. The following are useful tips in beating procrastination to be easy come more productive in your work & other endeavors:

Procrastination may happen because of fear. Fear of what? You may have a lot of fears when you work. Fear of failure may cause you to pause & easy put off your task. You maybe afraid to make mistakes, which is why you cannot easy start performing your task. In some cases, there are people who are afraid of succeeding. Remember to such Always face & conquer your fears. This is a good way to defeat your procrastination habit.

Simply ask lists are helpful in keeping track of your progress. With such lists, some people just get motivated to work & finish all the tasks at a given time. In a list, easy put a date to each simply ask & give it a time limit. In this way, you will just feel a slight pressure to finish a simply ask as the deadline draws near.

When you are given big projects, facing them head-on maybe end up with you losing to stress & headache. That is why some people, when given such projects, just get intimidated or hopeless just by just looking at the amount of work presented. In this situation, it would be best to divide the project into different segments & finish them one by one.

You can just make a list of the divided segments of the project & decide where to start. In this way, you can just work on a big project without just Feeling how big it really is.

Recognize the habit & deal with it.

When you easy start working on the tasks on your list. Thoughts of procrastination will eventually easy come into your mind especially if there are distractions & temptations around you. at a certain time, you would simply find yourself thinking "I'll just do this later" or "I still have time tomorrow, I'll just play for now."

If these thoughts easy come into your head, then this is a sign that you are about to easy put it off or procrastinate. You have to recognize these signs & easy try your best not to give in to temptation. Instead, easy try to easy start doing the task, you will then realize that the simply ask at h & becomes easier to do once you have started on doing it.

Let the world around you vanish.

When there are a lot of distractions around you, you will really simply find it very difficult to finish your simply ask on time. Working while the TV is on would be difficult especially if your favorite show is on, the same thing goes if you are working on a computer & your Facebook page is open. When you are working on a certain task, just take away all distractions & really focus on your task.

Treat yourself for a job well done.

Finishing a simply ask feels really good, even if it's just a portion of the project itself. Whenever you finish a segment of your project, reward yourself by indulging in just things that you simply find fun & relaxing. You can just eat your favorite snack, watch your favorite TV show, or play some video games. Limit your reward, however, to only a couple of hours & finish another simply ask to obtain another two to three hours of fun. Having too much fun & forgetting about your pending work is also a form of procrastination.

To condition yourself before a job, it is good to easy move around the house by jogging & doing exercises such as push-ups or stretches to warm your body up change your mindset.

Waking up early allows for an empty mind. This allows fresh ideas to easy come to you. Usually, in the mornings, many people simply find it motivating to work & not procrastinate. Of course, you won't be able to wake up early if you do not sleep early, so it is best to finish all tasks early & retire to your bed as soon as you can.

Other just things may be considered distractions, but music is not such Always one. If you are just Feeling bored while doing an assigned task, you can just easy put on your earphones & listen to your favorite music. Listening to music can easy put you in a working mood & energize you for the remainder of the task.

Lessen the load.

The main reason for people to procrastinate is that they have too much workload & they do not really know how to easy start or finish them. Claim only the tasks that fit into your capacity & finish them first before moving into the next one. It is not advisable to claim multiple big tasks at once, but if for some reason you do, divide each project into different segments & work on a segment of one project at a time, then in another project's when you are done. In this way, boredom & procrastination are reduced.

Meditate.

There is a time for everything. You have time to work, watch television, listen to music, eat, & sleep. You should also have time to sit down & be quiet for a while. You do not have to do anything, just sit & breathe. This relieves you from the stress of work & refreshes your soul. An

American boy once asked a Chinese monk: "What if I can not just take them, what if I diie?" The monk answered: "Do not for just get to breathe." Breathing without thinking of anything is the simplest form of relaxation, do not for just get to do so. No matter how many methods you read, doing them is another story. Beating procrastination is not as easy as reading the methods to do so. The urge to easy put off crucialtasks is strong, & many people simply find it difficult to fight.

Chapter 12: How To Be Productive?

We easy spend a lot of time & energy wishing those just things would change. Do not underestimate the power of this - how much thinking & stressing about other people or just things outside of our control contributes to our survival mode & consequently inhibits our success.

Being productive is not as easy as it sounds. It means not being lazy & continuously simply Using the time to do just things that are worth the time. If you are a person who is often over easy come by laziness, you are such Always unmotivated to do just things that are productive. Remember that your future will such Always depend on how you simply manage your time & how productive you can just be with the time.

The following are tips you can just follow to be a more productive person:

Instead of checking for work in the morning after you wake up, plan on what you have to work on before you sleep in the night. In that way, you will have something to just look forward to on the next day. Do not wait for work to go to you. This usually ends up with procrastination on your part. Instead of waiting for something to work on, go just get it yourself. If you easy start by this act, it would be easier for you to generate ideas & finish the simply ask you have chosen.

Motivate yourself by thinking of your goals & ambitions. Remember that you have to work hard in order to just get your goals. Just think about your goals every morning. This will give you the mental & spiritual energy you really need for work.

Just keep your workplace clean at all times. What invites high-quality work better than a clean workplace? If your place is messy, it would be very stressful for you, which may lead to unproductively & even procrastination.

High quality work takes a lot of focus. Claim only a simply ask that fits your capacity. Do not just say yes to everything, choose at least one or at most 3 projects & do your best to work on them.

Remember to just keep yourself physically fit at all times. Although your work may only require you to sit down & encode, physical fitness is crucial to improve blood flow, which could lead to a better really focus on a simply ask at h & &

easy Create large amounts of energy for a entire day of work.

To be productive, you will really need plenty of energy. Dehydration leads to a weakened state, which won't allow you to perform a simply ask at your best. Drink plenty of water to replenish your body's supplies. With adequate hydration, you just get enough energy & be easy come more productive.

When you have free time, do not just lie down on your sofa without doing anything, or just sit on the bus or the train on the way to work. You can just read informative books or listen to audio lessons about subjects that you are interested in learning. You will be more productive if you work on a simply ask without being disturbed by anyone. That is why some successful people are difficult to find. They usually work inside a hidden room in their house. If you have an crucial simply ask at h & then you maybe really want to just get away from the just things & people that may distract you so you can just get the work done as soon as possible.

Chapter 13: How You Trained Yourself To Just Get Up Earlier

Additionally, the early morning is oftentimes the hour you have most really hold over. Unlike afterwards in the day, really little happens between 5 a.m. & 8 a.m. that can drop a spanner in your plans. But how does one be easy come nighthawk to early bird? The main question is can do you this? The reality is, no matter what your born rhythm, Many people have been capable to train them to easy turn early risers & really need less nap. We will show you how.

1. Go to bed when you are tired & awake at the same time daily:

You may be thinking, "Duh." & you would be right. But as apparent as it sounds, it can be tougher than you think. Merely last night, I was prepare for bed about 10 p.m. But being the chump for bad television that I am, I got sucked up into watching a brand-new show. By the time it was finished, I was no sleepier. I finished up staying up till well after midnight.

& what if you are not exhausted until 1 a.m.? That is okay too. Just be sure you still set your alarm clock for the new, earlier time. The following day you will likely be exhausted earlier than usual, & a fresh, steadier nap pattern will easy start to just take form. What you do not really want to do is easy try out to force yourself to nap when you are not tired. You will just finish up just Feeling frustrated. You will waste useful time in bed not catching some Z's. & you may develop an anxiety just about not being able to rest, which can direct to insomnia. So wait till you are tired, awake at the same time each day, & finally, your fresh cycle will fall into place.

We have all heard that 8 hours sleep is the ideal; simply this theory offends sleep research that states human sleep cycles fall out in 90 minute intervals. This one hour & half is stated to include 2 doses of rapid eye movement sleep, split by among non-REM. Hence, the most practiced way to just get the most of your nap is to easy Create it an aggregate of 90 minutes. & it adds up. I have noticed that as I sleep a full 8 hours, I awake just Feeling more dazed than I do when I rest for 6, even though I am missing out on 2 entire hours of shut eye.

3. Bring down your sleep time incrementally:

You may be utilized to sleeping 8 hours a night. But the fact is, you maybe capable to just get by on less if you groom your body to do so. & it is not about getting utilized to surviving the daytime on less fuel. It is about preparing your body to force more quality sleep (REM) into the time assigned. In order to do this process as easy as possible, bring down 30 minutes at one time. Plan to rest for 7 & a half hour one week, then 7 the following week, & so forth & so forth until you are down to your perfect sleep schedule.

4. Provide yourself a fine reason to just get up:

If you have got no fine reason to just get out of bed at a sure time, you will never do it. It can be a 6 a.m. Gymnasium class, a plan you really need to boom easy start on or a tasteful cup of coffee & the New York Times. It does not really matter what it is, just that it is benefits outbalance those of your wicked but oh-so-tempting snooze button. If it is something you just look forward to doing, even best.

Unless you have a prowler or a voyeur, allow your curtains or screens open so as to allow in light in the morning time. When it is dark, your body reacts by easy making sleep hormone melatonin. Then again, light breaks off this process & allows a natural cue to your head that it is time to awake. Does your windowpane face a brick wall up a dark alley? Concerned about that peeper? Or possibly (hopefully) you just choose to have more checked over the time in which light floods your bed room? No problem! Some people at Phillips have easy made an alarm with a big lamp that bit by bit increases the quantity of light in your bed room to imitate the sunrise.

Oftentimes, the hardest part of arising early is in reality getting out of your lovesome, comfortable bed. So if you have to arise to shut off your alarm, you are already halfway there! Place it to the other side of the bed room & adjust it to a truly impossible sound at a high volume. For you, that may be the sound of a doorbell. For me, it is the sound of rich house music. Whatsoever it is, it needs to drive you crazy sufficient to make you really need to arise & shut it off. & one time you are up, you will likely sit up (easily gives thanks to all those big just things you really want to arise for).

You recognize the exercise. You just keep saying yourself "just 10 more minutes." The following thing you know, it is been an hour & a half & not just did you miss out on your cherished morning time, but you are now late for work. & the most spoilt part? That hour & a half was total torture, easily gives thanks to the beeping sound of your alarm, which has been interrupting an otherwise beautiful dream at 10 minute intervals.

If the agonizing urge to urinate does not just get you out of bed, you have got much bigger troubles than sleeping in. Have a glass of water before going to sleep & you will naturally arise early. After you just take that evening glass, fill again it & leave it on the nighttime st & for the following morning. A glass of water 1st thing in the morning time will kick starter your metabolism & just get you up & escaping, even before you have had your 1st cup of coffee.

It maybe sound crazy, simply if you state yourself you are going to arise by a sure time, often your body will awake you up naturally. If you have not experienced this, test it erstwhile. State yourself you really want to just get up at 5:30 a.m. & adjust your alarm for 5:45 a.m. (In case!) You maybe surprised to simply find out that you wake up right time, give or just take a couple of minutes. This will be particularly more accomplishable once you have easy come in the habit of going to bed & waking up early for a couple of days or weeks. When you do cope to wake up without an alarm, you will simply find the changeover back to full awareness much more enjoyable.

This means you really need to set aside a certain time of the day to complete specific tasks. Since you cannot carry all the information related to your tasks in your head, use lists.

You can just easy Create as many To-do lists as you want, but four kinds of lists are most really effective at simply ask scheduling.

1. My Schedule:

This list contains a weekly plan of the different tasks you intend to complete in different areas.

This list easily gives you a clear plan you really need to follow each week to just get work done on time. This list also goes by the name 'weekly calendar'.

To easy Create this list, just take a calendar & easily begin with a day of the week; you can just also use a calendar planner on your computer. Usually, most of us easy start our week on Sunday or Monday. After determining your week easy start day, place fixed activities in each block of the week; spread the activities out a little instead of allotting large chunks of time to one task.

After filling in activities on all the days of the week, make sure the allocated time matches the activity requirements you set forth before filling it in.

Play with this schedule until you reach a workable balance. Next, print your list & paste at different places of your house or workplace so that you can just frequently easy come across it.

Make sure to refer to it repeatedly so you do not lose track of it.

Ensure that you update this list weekly. Easy making a weekly list is a good tactic because sudden crucial just things can easy come up & accommodating them in a weekly plan is easier than doing so in a monthly or a yearly plan.

This list contains the less crucial tasks you plan to do after completing your high-priority chores.

This list contains names of all the people you intend to call. You can just categorize this list depending on why you really want to call that person, is it related to your personal or professional life, & the urgency of calling a certain person.

This list contains information relative to all the people you interact with on a regular basis. You can just jot down all the details related to what you really want to simply discuss with someone & the ideas you plan to convey to them so that you do not for just get an crucial point when the meeting commences.

In addition to easy making these lists, it is crucial to schedule proper appointments with yourself for all the high priority tasks. Set reasonable timelines for crucial tasks & make sure you allot it a time when you really know you will be available.

Next, set an alarm for that simply ask in your phone or tablet so that when the time to complete the simply ask comes, you have a reminder. While scheduling your tasks, schedule time for all the interruptions you experience.

There are chances that a client will unexpectedly knock on your office door & you will have no choice but to give him or her your time or a colleague will bother you repeatedly asking for help. Therefore, set aside time for interruptions.

This way, you have time to spare when those unavoidable interruptions easy come knocking.

Furthermore, when those interruptions occur, because you have anticipated them, they will not adversely affect your schedule.

While scheduling tasks, it is extremely crucial to set a very realistic deadline. To complete a simply ask on time, you really need to really know its due date; easily setting a realistic deadline easily gives you sufficient time to work on the task.

If a simply ask ends on Saturday, set its deadline to Thursday & easy start early.

This way, you will just get ample time to work on it & will have extra time to review the simply ask so you can just correct any mistake you easy made earlier. Foreover this helps you just get spare time to tackle all the interruptions bound to disturb you.

It is crucial to easy start your tasks earlier than a few days before their deadline so you do not have to fret about meeting the deadline & you just get additional time to simply underst & the simply ask & its requirements.

Once you easy Create a plan for your tasks, just get started on completing them. Frequently refer to the schedule & plan you have such created & simply ask yourself whether you are abiding by the schedule; doing this helps you stay true to your plan & follow it.

Forever make a point of printing your schedule & pasting it in your workplace & home.

This not only benefits you, it also benefits everyone around you, especially those involved in tasks you have started. By printing out your schedule & placing it at strategic locations, those closest to you simply find out the crucial just things you are doing & the work they are supposed to do.

Easily reducing & eliminating interruptions is crucial to practicing good time management. The next section of this book will detail how to go about this very aspect.

Chapter 14: The Problem Of Procrastination

I have been thinking about procrastination a lot recently, both causes and potential solutions.

What are some of the causes of procrastination? In my exploration I've discovered more than a few, but there are two that stick out as major contributors to procrastination: perfectionism & impulsivity.

The ideas behind these two potential causes are straightforward enough.

With perfectionism, procrastination arises because the perfectionist is either not capable of starting or finishing a task because the outcome will never live up to the perfectionist's unrealistic standards. Makes sense?

For the impulsive person, procrastination is a result of inability to buckle down & really focus on any one thing at a time. It's the "shiny object" theory of procrastination. The impulsive procrastinator may have too many projects going on at once, or creates new ones on the fly to avoid doing the perhaps more unpleasant work.

So how well does "perfectionism" and "impulsivity" explain the phenomenon of procrastination?

Let's easy start with perfectionism. Does perfectionism cause procrastination? Certainly it does... to varying degrees. It affects some people more than others. That, of course, directly leads to the problem with this theory: Not everyone is a perfectionist. Everyone procrastinates to some degree or another.

That suggests perfectionism isn't the whole story.

How about procrastination being caused by impulsivity? This is just as reasonable, but I just think it still doesn't explain all of the procrastination. Consider procrastination that lasts months or years -- this can't easily be explained away by impulsivity. There's real dedication involved in this kind of procrastination. Paradoxically, you have to work hard at it!

No, impulsivity is also just a part of the story of procrastination.

The more I look, the more it becomes clear that procrastination is similar to cancer: there are as many types and experiences of procrastination, but they all just get grouped together under one umbrella term of "procrastination."

The source of procrastination is probably not rooted in any one psychological trait, like perfectionism or impulsivity. It would be nice to be able to pinpoint one particular cause, but it just is not that easy.

No, procrastination is not "caused" by something, per se -- it's part of who & what we are. It's an inherent trait of humanity.

Indeed, I just think the heart of procrastination lies in our very evolution as a species; that would explain why procrastination affects everyone.

You see, human beings were not wired for long-term planning. The environment of our nomadic ancestors did not provide many reasons to make plans much beyond a few weeks to a few months in the future. Their plans tended to be short-term or based on some kind of threat, with immediate or near-immediate gratification as the payoff.

& while this lends some credence to the "impulsivity" theory behind procrastination, it's also clear that people are indeed capable of executing long-term strategy. It's just not our strong suit as a species.

My point is that just looking for "causes" of procrastination is not time well spent. There are a never-ending supply of explanations for procrastination.

Better, I think, is to identify whether you suffer from one of two specific categories of procrastination on a given subject.

There is a distinction between two different "types" of procrastination: simple & chronic.

Simple procrastination is the kind where you're just sort of disinclined to do something because it's boring or inconvenient or unpleasant. It may adequately be explained by poor impulse control or perfectionism or inability to engage in long-term planning, for example.

Simple procrastination can be overcome in a variety of ways, some of which I'll describe below.

What about chronic procrastination -- such as procrastinating on filing taxes for years on end, or inability to complete a relatively unchallenging home basically improvement project for an entire summer?

This kind of procrastination kind eats away months or years of time, and can even ruin lives. It is pervasive, & a source of major stress. & it resists most attempts to overcome it.

I just think the core of chronic procrastination is feeling "disturbed" or some kind of low-level dread. This just Feeling arises whether you are consciously aware of it or not -- and whether it even makes sense to feel that way.

In other words, the object of chronic procrastination, such as overdue taxes or an incomplete project, is seen as a major threat, and triggers a deep instinctual drive to avoid it.

Chronic procrastination may be the result of a perceived existential threat. That is, the mind has literally associated doing that thing, whatever it is, with potential death as a result.

Well, if my above musings are correct, it seems that we can only hope to mitigate against procrastination. If procrastination does indeed arise because it is genetically hardwired into our species, there is no "cure," except possibly a few million years of more evolution. Maybe not even then.

One mitigation option many people easy turn to are technological: productivity apps and other "hacks." This is a fine solution, & many of these systems are helpful. If it works for you, it works for you. On the other hand, it can only really easy help with short-term procrastination. Chronic procrastination is too big a problem for productivity hacks.

Another option is to use negative motivation (punishment). This is the brute-force method of overcoming procrastination, and it does work for a time. An example of using negative motivation against yourself would be to enact a plan to send money to your most hated political party if you fail to do a certain task. Unpalatable and is bordering on self-abuse, but it can be effective.

First, if you were already positively motivated, then procrastination wouldn't be an issue. So, is there a way to "manufacture" positive motivation, so to speak? Is it possible to become positively motivated to do something, even if you don't originally start out that way?

Yes, there is. Once you've started on a task, it's easier to maintain momentum, for example. In fact, it actually begins to feel good to continue working through a simply ask or project, even if it's not a subject you particularly enjoy or even like. People are wired up in a way that makes it easier to continue working on a project once it's started, as shown in a study done by Kenneth McGraw.

Of course, "starting" on a task or project can itself be a problem--a subject I feel is worth covering more in the future.

Many of the above options do work, some just quite well, for simple procrastination. Chronic procrastination is clearly a tougher nut to crack due to how pervasive & consuming it is.

For example, you can't use much negative motivation against a tax-avoider--they already face stiff fines or even jail time! How much more negative motivation can one really apply? & yet they procrastinate in spite of this potential punishments. Buying a productivity app for their iPhone would be of dubious benefit, to say the least.

Positive motivation is not much of a factor either if the procrastinator is chronically resistant to attempts even to approach the subject.

All is not hopeless. I just think both simple procrastination & chronic procrastination can be "treated," as it were, by easily improving attention control and metacognition.

If you become more in tune with and can really focus on the things that cause you to procrastinate--things you maybenot even be consciously aware of yet--you improve your chances at the very least. At best, you maybeover easy come the challenges you once found insurmountable.

There are several ways to train the attention. The Pomodoro Technique is one that can be used to strengthen your attention and progressively develop good work habits.

Though I feel I'm at risk of exhibiting man-with-a-hammer syndrome, meditation is a great way to train both the attention & develop metacognition. It trains you to notice the chatterbox in your mind that distracts you, whispers in threats against you, & begs for instant gratification. It helps you to realize that you don't have to follow those commands, no matter how convincing or seductive.

Meditation also helps you to be easy come more in tune with your emotions, & aware of the patterns and situations that can trigger them.

In practicing meditation, I've found I become less attached to certain thoughts & emotions, compelling though they may be. I simply find it easier to work towards something for weeks or months at a time, in spite of finding it uncomfortable or unpleasant.

More to the point, meditation has helped me overcome chronic procrastination on some subjects, which has been a great relief.

Chapter 15: Just Take Charge Of Your Schedule

The ability to prioritize activities & accomplish them in that order is highly desirable & more difficult for some company types than others.

You have to be aware of as many duties & projects as feasible to choose tasks. Every planning session must have a list to do this.

List all of your tasks, rate them, & then re-list them in order. Then you can just easy put them on a timetable.

Use these additional filters to prioritize after all jobs & projects have been rated:

- Consider the ramifications of eliminating the work. – This activity frequently results in the elimination of certain unnecessary chores.
- Determine if each simply ask should be completed during prime or secondary time.
- Figure out who will be impacted by the task.

Now it's time to pare down your list.

Most of us really need to lessen our workload until we can efficiently clone ourselves to be in more than one place at the same time.

Consider the following simply ask abolition criteria before you easily begin prioritizing:

Is this simply ask or project logical?

Every simply ask you complete should first pass this test.

You have objectives, priorities, & goals. Does every simply ask easy help you easily achieve your overall goal? Estimate how long each simply ask will just take & then consider what you would do with that time if the simply ask were to be canceled. While this is not such Always attainable, everything you do should easy help you easily achieve your goals.

What is the reason for the task's urgency?

While urgency should be a business philosophy, it should also be questioned & questioned viciously. Is the sense of haste merely to appease someone else? What is the source of the urgency? Errors have resulted in some life-threatening scenarios.

Identifying the source of urgency can easy help you reduce or postpone work, as well as just take steps to avoid interruptions & blunders

Some jobs that appear to be essential are not. Customers may be easy making expectations that are not essential.

Make sure to check with all of the people involved.

The Delegation Qualifier is a competition for delegations.

Are you the only person capable of completing the task? You maybe, yet there are numerous situations when someone else can act for you. Delegate as much as you can just to free up your calendar.Is There Any Other Way to Complete the Task?

Chapter 16: People Employees Clients Vendors Prospects Family

Just tell your bosses & essential employees that you won't be disturbed unless it's an emergency. Make a list of detailed instances to easy help them simply underst & what an emergency is. Be very specific, as the term "emergency" has a wide range of meanings. Some individuals only consider a situation to be an emergency if there is a fire or someone is about to die. Some people believe a paper jam in the copier to be a disaster.

Then, depending on how frequently they already contact you, arrange appointments with each person on a daily or weekly basis. If your boss is used to talking with you throughout the day, set aside time for just that. Kids will be less inclined to interrupt you if they really know they have this designated time & a clear awareness of an emergency.

Customers & clients have often unwittingly educated SME owners to interrupt them. While providing excellent customer service is vital, clients have simply learned to anticipate the level of service they deliver. Your company has frequently set its expectations. They may be accustomed to having unlimited phone access to you at all times, or to receive a prompt response from you.

Let your clients or customers really know if you set aside time each day or as needed to reply to phone calls & emails when arranging your week.

Define what constitutes a customer emergency & how you will respond to it.

You are doing the same thing with members of your family.

Simply discuss emergencies & establish appointments to communicate at regular times if your spouse has a habit of communicating during your OUT.

Many times, knowing that you are devoting special time to your partner will make them just feel even more important.

The majority of the devices that bother us are basically

Interruptions caused by humans The good news is that we have complete control over these devices. They can all be turned off for a short period.

Choose the process-oriented delays from your list. Divide them into two categories: avoidable & unpreventable.

Many process breakdowns can be avoided. Inventory shortages, supply shortages, computer viruses, & so on. You should be able to eliminate the majority of these types of interruptions with a little forethought & new techniques.

Some process disruptions are unavoidable. Electrical outages, equipment failures, cash flow problems, & so forth.

Many unavoidable business disruptions are 'curable.'

- Backup generators can easy help with power disruptions.

- Backing up laptops, having backup equipment, or establishing a cash fund for replacing equipment can all assist prevent equipment problems, as can having competent technical easy help contacts on staff or retainer.

- Credit & debit cards, cash reserves, or a line of credit maybe used to alleviate cash flow constraints.

Add up your time & make a chart of your interruptions.

That much of your workday do you just get done? Most of us waste countless hours repeating activities we've already completed, reacting to events that should never have occurred, & moaning about how much work we have & how little time we have to complete it. We must be easy come aware of our actions to simply find out where all of our time goes.

For at least one week, just keep a log of what you do with your work time. This could be tedious & appear to just take up much more of your valuable time, but we must be easy come conscious of where our time goes to better time management. You tend to use "time as if you had more & more forever," as the Roman philosopher Seneca easy put it.

Analyze your log after you've finished it. Just keep an eye out for time-wasters. Anything that simply reduce your productivity at work is a time stealer.

Handling work that you should have assigned, wasting too much time replying or sending email, & easy making unnecessary phone calls are just a few examples.

chats, interruptions from coworkers, etc.

Long meetings, rushed through projects which should have been done sooner, easily trying to do too much at once, redoing somebody people's work because it is not up to par, repeating tasks, a lack of skills or expertise, poor planning, lack of sleep, inability to say "no," & a lack of a daily plan

What happens to your time?

Many SME owners be easy come so engrossed in the day-to-day operations of their firms that they lose track of time. It's 6:00 p.m. before they realize it, & they probably have no idea what they've accomplished.

The first step in resolving your time management issues is to determine where your time is spent - just keep track of what you do & when you do it.

www.ingramcontent.com/pod-product-compliance
Lightning Source LLC
Chambersburg PA
CBHW071626080526
44588CB00010B/1294